Paul Weller Stanley Road

Wise Publications
London / New York / Paris / Sydney / Copenhagen / Madrid

Exclusive Distributors:

Music Sales Limited
8/9 Frith Street, London W1V 5TZ, England.

Music Sales Pty Limited
120 Rothschild Avenue, Rosebery, NSW 2018, Australia.

Wise Publications
Order No. AM933141
ISBN 0-7119-5233-7
This book © Copyright 1995 by Wise Publications.

Music arranged by Roger Day.
Music processed by Paul Ewers Music Design.

Your Guarantee of Quality:

As publishers, we strive to produce every book to the highest commercial standards.

Whilst endeavouring to retain the original running order of the recorded album,
the book has been carefully designed to minimise awkward page turns and to make playing from it a real pleasure.

Particular care has been given to specifying acid-free,
neutral-sized paper made from pulps which have not been elemental chlorine bleached.
This pulp is from farmed sustainable forests and was produced with special regard for the environment.

Throughout, the printing and binding have been planned to ensure a sturdy,
attractive publication which should give years of enjoyment. If your copy fails to
meet our high standards, please inform us and we will gladly replace it.

Music Sales' complete catalogue describes thousands of titles and
is available in full colour sections by subject, direct from Music Sales Limited.
Please state your areas of interest and send a cheque/postal order for £1.50 for postage to:
Music Sales Limited, Newmarket Road, Bury St. Edmunds, Suffolk IP33 3YB.

Printed in the United Kingdom by
Halstan & Co Limited, Amersham, Buckinghamshire.

The changingman.

Words by Paul Weller
Music by Paul Weller & Brendan Lynch

Verse 2:
Our time is on loan
Only ours to borrow
What I can't be today
I can be tomorrow.

Bridge 2:
And the more I see
The more I know
The more I know
The less I understand.

Bridge 3: (%)
And the more I see
The more I know
The more I know
The less I understand.

Porcelain gods.

Words & Music by Paul Weller

1. Be-ware false pro-phets,   take a stand!___   My for-tune cook-ie
(Verses 2 & 3 see block lyric)

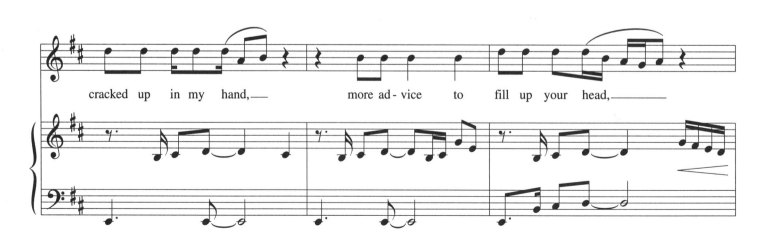

cracked up in my hand,___   more ad-vice   to   fill up your head,___

more emp-ty words— from the liv-ing— dead—

who seek and ex-plain— what can't real-ly be said.—

CHORUS

——— And how dis-ap-point-ed— I— was—

to turn out— af-ter all,— just a

por - ce - lain god that shat - ters when it falls.

1.

N.C.

2. Too much will kill you,
(See block lyric)

mp

2.

too lit - tle ain't e - nough,

When it

falls.

f

my for-tune cook-ie cracked in my hand.

Repeat to fade

Segue to 'I Walk On Gilded Splinters'

Verse 2:
Too much will kill you, too little ain't enough
You shout my name but I'll call your bluff
Most who see me, see me not for real
We fake and fawn, play games 'til dawn
But I could see what you can see
And I hate too, what you hate in me.

Chorus 2:
And how disappointed I am
To find me part of no plan
Just a porcelain god
That shatters when it falls.

Verse 3: (D.C.)
I shake it off and start again
"Don't lose control" I tell myself
Life can take many things away
Some people will try and take it all
They'll pick off pieces as they watch you crawl.

Chorus 3:
And how disappointed I am
To find me part of no plan
Just a porcelain god
That shatters when it falls.

I walk on gilded splinters.

Words & Music by Dr. John Creaux

♩=88

N.C.

mf

N.C.

1. Some

℅ VERSE 1

N.C.

peo-ple think they're jam-my but I know they must be cra-zy,
(Verse 3 (℅) see block lyric)

can't see their mis-for-tune ev-en if they're cra-zy.

BRIDGE

Kon, kon, the kid-dy kon, kon, walk on gild-ed splint-ers,_____

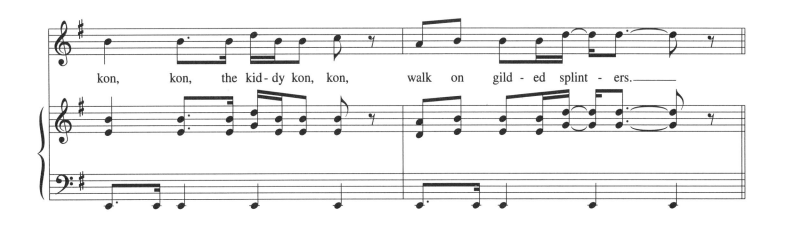

kon, kon, the kid-dy kon, kon, walk on gild-ed splint-ers._____

N.C.

To Coda ⊕

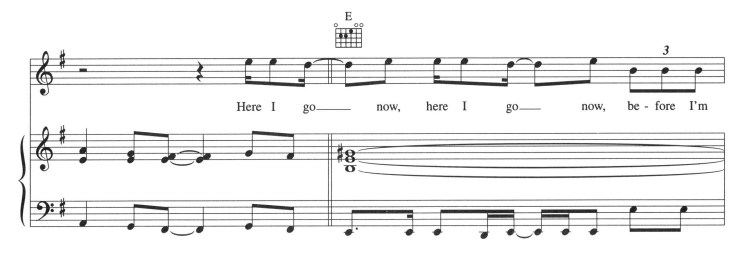

E

3

Here I go_____ now, here I go_____ now, be-fore I'm

dead. Be-fore I'm dead,— here I go— now, here I go— now, 'til I'm dead.— I

N.C.

rode out my cof-fee by drink-ing poi-son from— my cha-lice,

D.%. al Coda

propped a-gainst— my faith— I drink oil for my ma - lice.

⊕ Coda

'Til I'm dead.——

Verse 3:
Meet me on the doorstep
Soon we'll be in the gutter
Melting just like butter
How come I make you stutter

Verse 4: (as Verse 2)

Bridge:

Chorus:

You do something to me.

Words & Music by Paul Weller

won - der - ful_____
(Verse 3 instrumental to chorus)

then chase_ it all_ a - way,_

mix - ing my_ e - mo -

- tions,_____

that throws_ me back_ a - gain._

Hang - ing on the

Woodcutters son

Words & Music by Paul Weller

1. Su - gar - town,— — yeah,— has turned so sour,— — its peo - ple ang-

(Verses 2 & 3(𝄋) see block lyric)

-ry   in their sleep.___   There's more small-

___ town,   mm, pa - ra - noi - a___   sweep-ing down___

its   ev - il   streets.___

Give me a chance,___   I'll cut you down with a   glance,___   yeah, with

cut - ting down the wood for the good of ev - ery - one._____

Play 3 times

D.%. al Coda

Piano solo ad lib.

3. There's a si -

⊕ *Coda*

I'm

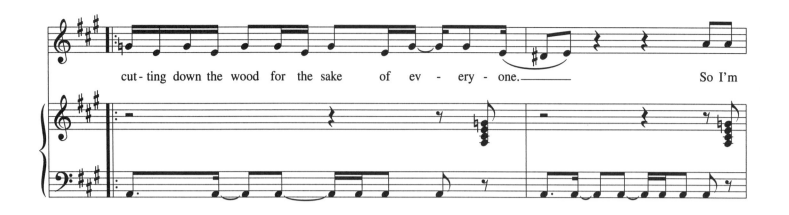

cut - ting down the wood for the sake of ev - ery - one._____ So I'm

Piano ad lib. to fade

cut - ting down the wood for the sake of ev - ery - one._____ I am

Verse 2:
You can tell it's witching hour
You can feel the spirits rise
When the room goes very quiet
And there's hatred in their eyes.

Verse 3: (𝄋)
There's a silence when I enter
And a murmur when I leave
I can see their jealous faces
I can feel the ice they breathe.

Time passes...

Words & Music by Paul Weller

hard   to   trace_____   these   feel - ings._____

quick - ly.

4. The

fi - nal stage, we've both reached some way, as we

board our trains to differ-ent sta - tions. And these

Verse 2:
Gone so soon, the time I spent with you
And like an old, old tune keeps running through my head
I wanted to say so many things
But my mouth went dry and one word and I'd cry.

Stanley road.

Words & Music by Paul Weller

1. A ha-zy mist hung down the street, the length of its mile
(Verse 2 see block lyric)

Verse 2:
The summer nights that seemed so long
Always call me back to return
As I re-write this song
The ghosts of night, the dreams of day
Make me swirl and fall and hold me
In their sway

And it's still in the distance
And it shines like the sun
Like silver and gold
It goes on and on
It goes on and on
It goes on and on
It goes on and on.

Broken Stones.

Words & Music by Paul Weller

ken stones— we're all try-ing to get— home.—

2. Like a lo-ser's reach— too slow and short to hit the peaks,

yeah,— so lost— and a-lone,—

yeah, try-ing to— get home.— As an-oth-er bit

To Coda

yeah,_____ he's lost_____ and a - lone,_____

yeah, like bro - ken stones._____

And an - oth - er bit

BRIDGE 2

shat-ters,   oh, an-oth-er lit-tle bit gets___ lost.___

Tell me what else real-ly mat-ters,___   oh,___ at such a

cost._____   4. Like peb - bles on a

D.%. al Coda

⊕ *Coda*

Try - ing to get home,   try - ing to get

46

Out of the sinking.

Words & Music by Paul Weller

1. Past mid-night's hold,— where the world's a-wait-ing,—
(Verse 2 see block lyric)

— I'll wait for— your love.—

will take us a - way._____

will take us a - way,_____

and there we will—— stay._____

But I can't find the key.—

Verse 2:
Late at night
When the world is dreaming
Way past the stars
That ignore our fate
And all twinkle too late to save us
So we save ourselves.

Chorus 2:
Hey baby do just what you're thinking
Know I know it, yeah, feel I'm sinking
Know I feel it, I know you feel it too
Across the water there's a boat that will take us away.

Chorus 3: (%)
Out of the sadness, far from the madness
Into sunlight, out of the sinking
You know I feel it, I know you feel it too
Across the water there's a boat that will take us away
And there we will stay.

Pink on white walls.

Words & Music by Paul Weller

And the sun shone

And the sun shines pink on my wall, and the

Verse 2:
Yeah, when it comes, it comes quick!
An' when you're least expecting it
But the top's the bottom
An' the bottom is all you got.

Verse 3:
When it comes, it comes quick!
When you're least expecting it
But the top's the bottom
The bottom's all you got.

Whirlpools' end.

Words & Music by Paul Weller

children choking on a poison cloud,—

while on the streets where lovers once walked,— side by side in
(Verse 2 (𝄋) see block lyric)

i - dle talk.— Bul - lets fall like un - ho - ly rain,—

peo - ple change as the pa - nic sets in.— A fright-ened ba - by by her

dead moth-er's side,___ in a bru-tal world where there's

no-where to run,___ hide___ or___ cry.___ Now noth-ing

BRIDGE

feels the same___ way,___
(Bridge 2 see block lyric)

feel like I'm chang-ing a-gain,___ up-on a

ov - er____ our heads but   far e - nough___ to see.____

Guitar solo ad lib.

Guitar solo ad lib.

2 bar drum break

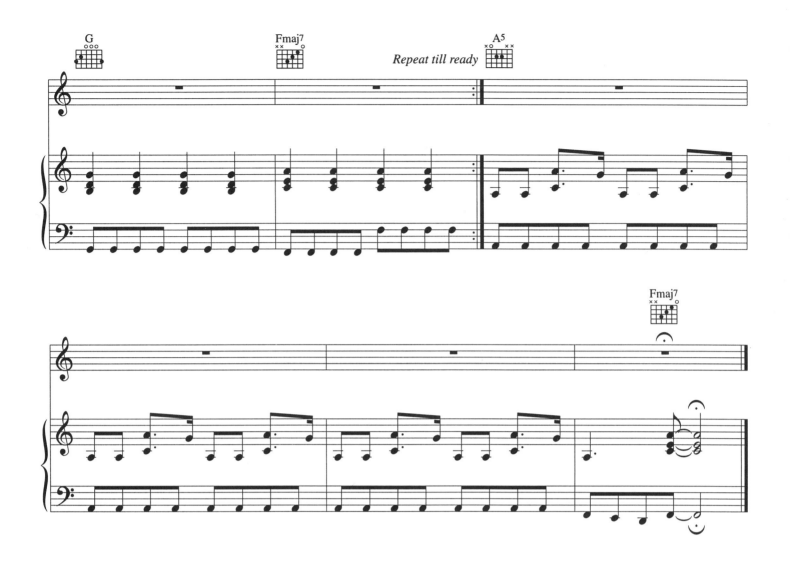

Verse 2 (%):
I ran as fast as my feet could fly
Down country lanes where I took my time
Time like a hound snapping at my heels
I got past thinking so that I could feel
Feels like a film playing in my head
I kept on rolling down green Surrey hills in spring.

Bridge 2:
Now I don't feel the same way
Feel like I'm changing again
Upon a street with no name
It's hard to find me again.

Wings of speed.

Words & Music by Paul Weller

1. 3.(%) Fly on wings of speed that will bring you home to me,

(Verse 2 see block lyric)

I'll ne - ver be free

To Coda ⊕

from the dark - ness I _____ see, _____ as I wait for your _____

_____ smile.

Choir

Verse 2:
Though my hands are tied
My feet are bound by fate
With clay at the base
As I sit and wait
What visions I see.

9/96 (25724)